FRAMELESS

TESHELLE COMBS

Teshelle Combs Books

Copyright © 2020 by Teshelle Combs

Manufactured in the United States of America.

Book layout and design by Nate Combs Media.

ISBN-13: 979-8609960030

For the courage of the overlooked
and the subtleties of the overloved.

FRAMELESS

TESHELLE COMBS

Black

I am the full.

I do not need to dare you

To find anything more whole.

I am not greed-filled

In my consumption.

What I bring is in itself

Complete.

I swallow the main and the excess

In gentle motions

Or all at once.

Midnight

The beginning or the ending

From the perspective of

Painters and prayers.

I am not to be captured,

But to be witnessed...

And you with

Heads uplifted

And pupils dilated,

Searching for something else—

For anything else—

But finding only

Yourself

In

Me.

Ebony

Slick and wet.

Dark is not my way;

I am deeper still.

And with a purpose.

To show that even

The void can be

Fluid

When it is allowed

To be.

Charcoal

Utility is mine

Even if you think

It's yours.

You grip me in fingers and scrape me with paper.

You stoke me with branches and light me on fire.

But it is I who allow

You to use

The thickness

Of me.

Obsidian

Jagged and glistening.

I am sharp edges

When I could be curves.

You did not believe

A color could kill

Until I showed you.

Pitch

I offer a solution.

That otherness is meant

For others.

That I do not violate

My nature

In sharing it with the light.

That I can be me

And I can be you.

That darkness can

Bring light

And fire can be found.

Gray

I am not ashamed

Of being both and

Being neither.

I am not alarmed

Nor dismayed

For what they say

Or fail to say

Of me.

I am not wild

Nor bold

Nor demanding

Nor negating.

But I am risking.

I am forgiveness—

Both and yet...both.

Ash

The awe of effect.

Never dismal.

More of a shifting

Admiration.

I am come from

What has gone.

But still...

How lovely.

Flint

You are unaware of me.

Your eyes cannot see

The value or the valor.

Unless your hands

Have been taught

That I am for beginnings.

The most ordinary

Brings the most brilliant blaze

If it is not overlooked.

Slate

You want me blank

But it is not what I want.

I am only little so I can hold much.

Come put yourself upon me.

All your many selves.

I will not compete.

I will not comply.

I will collaborate.

Smoke

Motion is mine.

I spiral, twist

And I rise.

See me in the distance,

Changing and using my time

To make my message known:

That something is coming

Or something is dying

Or something once was

And isn't anymore.

I cannot be caught.

I cannot be kept.

I will be remembered

In fleeting memories

And dreams of dread.

Pewter

Things are made by me.

You see me finished

And for you.

This is well and good.

Though you use me,

You do it well,

With attention

And hunched over

My details.

I would rather be pained

Than plain.

Brown

I am wealth.

From me is the growth of all things.

I receive and I give

In abundance.

If ever I am unnoticed,

It is because you are made of me.

Your skin,

Your hair,

Your eyes.

You cannot be apart from me.

I am you.

Coffee

I am for spilling.

Into mouths.

Onto paper.

I am a giver.

You have always been a taker.

Yet you give me your love

When I give you

Obsession.

I am nothing to look at

Except that I am

What you want.

Cinnamon

Fall in love

With the grit of me.

The bits of red you cannot predict.

The burn of me.

I am richness and complication

And very well loved

For it.

Cedar

Call me common

But I am more backbone than background.

Delicate and never seeming to run out.

The beauty of me is in

How I can be everywhere

And no one seems to mind.

Umber

Luscious and righteous.

Don't you want to take

Pools of me into your hands?

Don't I make you believe

You could fashion a new race

If only you had more of me to manifest?

Beige

You think light of me.

I have blended in but not away.

I make a point, though softly:

You cannot have starkness

Without simplicity.

You cannot have solidity

Without support.

You

Need

Me.

I

Am

Here.

Bronze

I am more than one.

In the tucks and turns,

In the hills and valleys,

The light plays with me,

Revealing shadows

And reveling in shimmers.

One name does not always mean

One nuance.

Green

Reach for me

For I am always reaching.

My nature is growth.

My nature is growing.

I am not afraid of the exhale,

For I am its source.

I am always more than I appear

For I am always more.

Sage

Calmness comes to you.

A slow burn.

A sweet crease.

A gentle curl.

I do not bring.

I do not adjust.

I do not assume.

I only am

What you need

To stop trying to be

And be.

Olive

I come with undertone

That says I am not to be

Abandoned

Or ignored.

What beauty

In the truth I cradle—

Taste and see,

Hold and feel,

Offer and be freed.

I come

In peace.

Basil

Healing in a stroke of genius.

The scent of more than enough

For the whole family.

The sight of waiting

And then, when the time comes,

savoring.

Pine

Take comfort in knowing

My majesty is unending.

I am not the sort of nobility

To loom it over you.

I wear myself proudly and without ambition.

I am my own crown

And still I bless you

With needles for

Yours.

Seaweed

Murky and timeless.

You only know me through

The filter of churning waters.

But I have a secret

In the slip of my texture:

I have been here the whole time,

Holding up the rest

And ensuring you can breathe

Long enough to see

It.

Blue

Expanse and I share certain qualities

But I am more expansive than even that.

I am culmination. I am on and on.

I am wide openness.

Hallelujah to my horizons.

Search the sprawl of me

And you will have no choice

But to discover.

Denim

Hard work is no stranger to me.

I am familiar, spread against skin.

A rare one in my peasantry.

I love you enough to become like you,

Though I own most of everything—seas and summits and skies.

Instead, I will clothe you

With heaven's endurance

So you do not work

Alone

anymore.

Cobalt

I am both found and formed.

I give the illusion of elegance

But I am an earth-dweller.

The heat makes me

Undeniable.

I will take your breath

And leave you with

Beauty.

Indigo

I am the one

You want to lie in.

To cover your whole self with.

To become like.

To exist inside of.

You hope when you stare

Into me

You might find

You have become me.

Navy

Unnerving and unswerving.

You underestimate the power of

Officiality.

I am straight-backed and sharp-cornered.

I am authority understated.

Ocean

I am all the sun shines on.

Underneath and above.

The crest and the basin.

You are only a ripple in me—

Speckles under my control,

Afloat because I say so.

Goddess hue.

The footsteps of the Sovereign.

Origin Ourself.

Sky

Flit, float, or fly, but

I am soaring.

Above the sediment.

Beyond the breaking.

Eyes translate me to hints of freedom.

History in clouds—

Written in disappearing ink.

I have seen the whole of you

Though I have watched

And not interfered.

You come to me

But cannot touch me.

The flight and the plight

Are yours,

Not mine.

Purple

Honesty in grandeur

And unchanged over time.

I am an elixir

And you are scrambling for more of me.

I am the king. I am the queen.

You are the one who ends up

worn.

Plum

Frosted and supple.

Roundness on display

And for the taking.

Drip me. Smear me.

There is nothing else

But the sweetness of me.

Lilac

Unashamed fragility.

I am a scent untextured.

Deliberate and delicate.

A cadence whispered

Beneath hushed petals

And fluttering to meet you.

Lavender

Strength in my mothering.

Potent in the smooth strokes

And gathered on your behalf.

Bestowed on fields of green

And praised by cyan skies.

Hallowed in scent and

Renowned in the tint of my cure.

Pink

You think of me kindness

But I am coy.

Shy in my affect

But facading in my pigmentation.

I play simple, you see,

But I am surprising.

I act sweetly, you know,

But I am surmising.

Rose

I am the notion of unfolding.

Being closed in and trapped

And then unfurling to the touch of the sun.

Not by force do I yield,

But in my time, and with my light.

I am not on display

For your sake

But for mine.

Blush

Tint on the cheeks of the page.

The flush beneath lashes of the spiral bound.

Timid but not unsure.

More than fear. More than faint.

I am beckoning.

Kisses fading on bookmarks.

Unrequital left in the spaces between lines.

Red

Big.

Big and more and exactly enough

Without being too much.

All brash edges and wild wells.

Angles and turns and curves.

Spread wider than you can handle.

Sizzling and splashing.

Catch me, if you can.

You cannot.

But we both know you'll try.

Cherry

Flavor on the tip of a brush.

Finished in glaze and too sweet.

I am confidence.

I am an attempt to make a claim.

I am more than you can fit

In one bite.

Blood

Life.

Life and death.

I am a circle.

I am your circle.

Brick

I am human effort

Spread with palette knife

On primed canvas.

To see me is to touch me.

To touch me is to feel

The stories of slaves and slumber

Swelling through your fingertips

And building in your heart.

I am the color

Of home.

Scarlet

A deep cut.

A long thrill.

The sight of the hunt.

The wrapping of blood by the night.

A haunting song

Or a shallow grave.

And always

unashamed.

Wine

Hue of long nights

And late dinners.

Of miracles and

Monsters.

A bath in which to put the soul.

A long soak

And forgetting

And pretending it's

All going to be sweet.

Orange

Outstretched arms

And eyes for brimming.

The leap of the heart and

The set of the sun.

I am a laugh from the belly

Of Autumn.

I am a dance when the dawn cracks.

I am living

And being alive.

Rust

The crumbling of structure

And the bits and pieces of past utility.

Precautions untaken

And a slow comfort

In what you know happens

When you are not careful

To stay young.

Amber

Smooth and solace.

A slope away from pain and pressure.

A kind blend

Just when I am needed.

Pressed light to skin

And found in the stones of eyes.

Tiger

A rippling, stunning strength.

Motion in segmentation.

I hold the scepter and

You hold the senses.

I am beyond

And loudly so.

Ginger

Spice and prowess.

I am for grinding and spreading

And you are for mixing and storing.

Gold of the earth

And precious.

I am prestige

And you will

Enjoy me.

Honey

I am labor rewarded

And harvested at great cost.

Translucent yet rich.

Run me through your fingers

And into your mouth

And onto your canvas.

Yellow

Clever and clear.

At a distance,

I accent the world—

Bits of me interspersed to make magic.

Up close, I am intimacy.

I am slipping into your

Chest and your head

And bringing light.

I am light.

Gold

The power in me

Is in my ability to reflect.

You see in me

The image of yourself

Clothed in majesty

And rectified

And refined.

You fight for me—over ages and ages—

For the chance to seem

Better than you

Truly are.

Dandelion

Before I am useful,

I am beautiful.

I season sidewalks

With pops of hope—

A thread of a different tale

If you are paying attention:

Color for wishing

And wishing for color.

White

Vacuous and without end.

I am the void no one understands.

Complexity of too many

In one.

Anything but simple,

And everything but myself.

I am the vessel for

All the rest.

Pearl

Iridescence and elegance

Found in hidden places

And touched sparingly

To small spaces

In high homes,

Against the hollows

Of necks

Or the hollows

Of ancestry.

When I am perfect,

You are perfect.

Salt

Coarse for coarseness

And fine for fineness.

In every place and

In every way,

I am the truest pearl

Of the sea.

I am the course;

You are the consumer.

Rice

If you take the time

To look

Before you touch

And touch before

You take,

You can see

In me

The prism of

Standing knee deep in water

For generations come and gone.

I am a savior.

You would see

If you took

The time.

Lace

You see the delicate stitch

And marvel at the waves and ripples,

The webs and rings.

Have you noticed,

That I am as much

The thread

As I am its

Absence?

Bone

Brittle in dying

And brutal in living.

So much the whole point.

I house the flow of it all.

I am not iridescence or

Splashing

Or glistening.

I am not bold

Or bulging

Or birthing.

I am still

And still.

And I am for you

Thoughtlessly

And without remorse

And without

option.

More Works by Teshelle Combs

Let There Be Nine Series
- *Let There Be Nine Vol 1*: **Enneagram Poetry**
- *Let There Be Nine Vol 2*: **Enneagram Poetry**

For Series: Words laced together on behalf of an idea, a place, a world.

- **For Her**
- **For Him**
- **For Them**
- **For Us**

Love Bad Series: Poems About Love. Not Love Poems.

- **Love Bad**
- **Love Bad More**
- **Love Bad Best**

Standalone Poetry Books:

Breath Like Glass

Poems for love that never lasts.

Girl Poet

A collection of poems on the passion, privilege, and pain of being (or not quite being) a girl.

CORE SERIES

Ava is the kind of girl who knows what's real and what isn't. Nothing in life is fair. Nothing is given freely. Nothing is painless. Every foster kid can attest to those truths, and Ava lives them every day. But when she meets a family of dragon shifters and is chosen to join them as a rider, her very notion of reality is shaken. She doesn't believe she can let her guard down. She doesn't think she can let them in—especially not the reckless, kind-eyed Cale. To say yes to him means he would be hers—her dragon and her companion—for life. But what if Ava has no life left to give?

The System Series

1 + 1 = Dead. That's the only math that adds up when you're in the System. Everywhere Nick turns, he's surrounded by the inevitability of his own demise at the hands of the people who stole his life from him. That is, until those hands deliver the bleeding, feisty, eye-rolling Nessa Parker. Tasked with keeping his new partner alive, Nick must face all the ways he's died and all the things he's forgotten.

Nessa might as well give up. The moment she gets into that car, the moment she lays her hazel eyes on her new partner, her end begins. It doesn't matter that Nick Masters can slip through time by computing mathematical algorithms in his mind. It doesn't matter how dark and handsome and ir-resistibly cold he is. Nessa has to defeat her own shadows. Together and alone, Nick and Nessa make sense of their senseless fates and fight for the courage to change it all. Even if it means the System wins and they end up...well...dead.

Contact Teshelle Combs

Instagram @TeshelleCombs

Email: teshellecombs@gmail.com

Acknowledgments

Thank you to the teachers of the arts. The ones who hold passion condensed in their palms and pass to the ones coming next. You make us see. Without you, we would be in darkness and clinging to silhouettes and shadows. Please, find courage and resilience. You are needed and you are loved beyond your knowledge.